T0110257

The Brittingham Prize in Poetry

Centaur

POEMS

Greg Wrenn

The University of Wisconsin Press

The University of Wisconsin Press

1930 Monroe Street, 3rd Floor

Madison, Wisconsin 53711-2059

uwpress.wisc.edu

3 Henrietta Street

London WC2E 8LU, England

eurospanbookstore.com

Printed in the United States of America

Library of Congress Cataloging-in-Publication Data

Wrenn, Greg.

Centaur / Greg Wrenn.

p. cm. — (The Brittingham prize in poetry)

Poems.

Includes bibliographical references.

ISBN 978-0-299-29444-1 (pbk. : alk. paper) — ISBN 978-0-299-29443-4 (e-book)

I. Title. II. Series: Brittingham prize in poetry (Series)

PS3623.R464C46 2013

811'.6—dc23

2012032696

For Christopher—we're joined

descend, surround, and dissipate the glare,
banish the break-bone fever

—Elizabeth Bishop, "Florida Deserta"

Contents

V.

x

Acknowledgments

I gratefully acknowledge the editors of the following publications in which
these poems, sometimes in considerably earlier versions, first appeared:

The American Poetry Review: "Retrospection in Hannibal, Missouri"
(Section 1 of "Thirteen Labors"; as "Retrospection in Hannibal")

AGNI Online: "First Contact" (Section 7 of "Thirteen Labors"), "Prayer at Ojai"

The Antioch Review: "Pontiff"

Beloit Poetry Journal: "Centaur" (except Section 3), "One of the Magi,"
Section 12 of "Virus" (as "Epithalamium")

Boston Review: Sections 1, 2, 13 of "Virus" (as "To the Virus,"
"Reuben on Joseph," "My Thomas," and "The Ray")

Center: Section 8 of "Virus" (as "At Keats' Grave Again")

Colorado Review: "Interactivity," "Lucid Spooning," "Marriage"
(Sections 2, 9, and 12 of "Thirteen Labors")

Crazyhorse: "Circumcision"

cream city review: "Detainment," "Detainment"
(Sections 3 and 11 of "Thirteen Labors")

FIELD: "Mindfulness," "Monogamy"
(Sections 4 and 10 of "Thirteen Labors")

Indiana Review: "Manger"

The Laurel Review: "Onto"

LIT: Section 3 of "Centaur" (as "My Therapist's Last Notes")

Memorious: "Brother on Brother"

New Orleans Review: "Mother of Light"

1999 Grolier Poetry Prize Annual: "Revision"

Pebble Lake Review: Section 5 of "Virus" (as "Easter Snapshot")

Pleiades: Section 14 of "Virus" (as "My Euryklea")

The Southern Review: "Burial," "Fresco," "South of Jacksonville," "Three Attempts at Understanding" (as "Three Attempts to Understand Suffering")

The Yale Review: "Promiscuity," "Self-Portrait as Robert Mapplethorpe"

Some of these poems appear in *Off the Fire Road* (Green Tower Press, 2009), which Kevin Prufer chose as the winner of the Midwest Chapbook Series Contest.

"Brother on Brother" was included in the *Best of the Net Anthology 2007*. In addition, "One of the Magi" appeared on *Verse Daily* on December 26, 2007, and "Pontiff" appeared on *Poetry Daily* on March 8, 2009.

"Centaur" was nominated for a Pushcart Prize in 2009.

For their support at critical junctures, I offer my thanks especially to Zac Addison, Rick Albarran, Robin Ekiss, Deja Gamig, Saskia Hamilton, Mo Jones, Gene McAfee, Annie Nugent, Bridget Rolens, Randy Smith, Jaime Snow, Scott Warren, and Andy Wiese.

Thank you, Mamo, Papo, Mother, Dad, and Tommy.

I'd also like to thank my teachers for their support and feedback: Mary Jo Bang, Eavan Boland, Henri Cole, Kenneth Fields, Jorie Graham, Linda Gregg, Ed Hirsch, Cynthia Hogue, Carl Phillips, W. S. Di Piero, D. A. Powell, Peter Sacks, Natasha Trethewey, Kerri Webster, and Kelli Wells.

Thank you, Terrance Hayes, for believing in this collection.

Finally, I would also like to record my deep appreciation for financial support from the Stanford Creative Writing Program and the English Department at Washington University in St. Louis. I'm also especially grateful for scholarships and fellowships from the Bread Loaf Writers' Conference as well as the English Department at Harvard University, the Stadler Center for Poetry at Bucknell University, the Vermont Studio Center, and the Spiro Arts Foundation. And Marianne Williamson, Kathy Mackey, Janet Hall, and Elizabeth Renfroe.

I.

Centaur

1.

Smelling manure, the humid
sharpness of rainforests
beyond his stables

and field, I got off the bus.
For three days, I'd fasted on deviled
eggs and honey, sipped

turmeric water—just following
his orders, my orthopedic
surgeon's. I'd ripped out

his ad from the back
of an almanac,
dog-eared on top of a friend's toilet:

Do You Believe In CENTAURS?

*You can rid yourself of burdensome footed legs:
Dr. D. Angel of Brazil now offering a revolutionary
surgical procedure to become a centaur. Be 0 & 1,
sleek & wise velocity. Risk-free.*

It spoke to me, as a relic
seems more holy
once taken from its locked case

and placed in one's palm.

2. Intake Form: Part D

Always felt dead
    from the navel down.
Some man touched me in the crib,

    warped my bones.

        Never could run

    like the other boys, those lithe
        cheetahs flying past the dugouts,

    the fence feathered with creeper.
My feet splay out like an emperor

    penguin's—I will them into straightness but turn around

        and still see fresh,
        angled prints in the sand. Please

    hoist my hips from my body into the heavens,

    hot engine lifted
    from propped-open hood . . .

        Cordless,
    immaculate sander,
        work my ilia.

        Invisible chiropractor,
        tune my ischia, each grateful pubis,
    shift my kneecaps inward,

    nudge those two pneumatic clams

    closer in the mud.

4

3. His Therapist's Last Notes: A Fragment

stolen from her office in Watertown, Massachusetts

marcus says he must   do it he must Δ; advised him of my concerns:
   1. another distraction from   abuse hist.   2. issue
          = sex addiction   ≠ correcting phys. "deformity"
       3. medically risky   hygiene in Brzl?
           4. centaurs   are lusty (from my reading)

4. Previous Interventions

To reawaken waist to feet,
I've tried Utthita Trikonasana,
Rolfing sessions, psychedelic

meditation retreats, pure stretches
of mindfulness spiked
with extracts of Yucatán moss—

all a bunch of
New-Age baloney.
I considered binding my feet,

having the bones
of my lower
limbs broken, re-set.

—Too Geisha-like,
too Golgothan.
I let many men culled

from cyberspace
crush and slide into me,
choke the backs of my thighs

like chicken throats, graze
and bite, grip my arches,
but it never worked.

5.

"I want to feel alive,"

I said three times
as I rapped on the door
with the greasy horsehead knocker.

The intercom crackled.
A long tone. A nurse's voice
wavered
and gained strength:

"Sit on the cushion
in the center of the fourth stable.
Close your eyes.
Your left lid will twitch
when your animal whinnies and puffs
its arrows of
longing toward you."

6.

           motes curling in barnlight
                cushion really low milking stool
                    in middle of long corridor
       fringed with fisher price toys hay
         I plunked down stalls
    seemed to rattle breathe as single
                mammal tightly collared

        promised grace wasn't shot
           bow never even strung arrows
               never whittled feathered
      had I tapped unwitting interspecies
             morse code LET NO ONE
       LOVE ME choose me
    soulhorse let's go home

8

Dr. Angel shook me.
Then shook my hand.
"Do not despair, Mar-quoose.
Let's be more practical.
They can be so . . .
stoooo-burn."
Rolling his eyes
far back into his head,

he whirled about,
stopping to point at Mister,
whose eyes shone
like new blacktop.
"I hear him crying
your name. He's homesick."

7. Surgery

Holding the mask
over my mouth, Dr. Angel coun ted down
in Portuguese with a Tuscan

accent, and I heard Mister
being rolled in
on a wonky cart. No doubt

he was on his side,
on a bed of dry ice,

fine Sharpie lines drawn
along his lower neck . . .

When I woke, strange
birds were grooming themselves on the window sill.
No saliva in my mouth.

I heard water running continuously.

An enormous drum of pain
persisted below my stomach, pinch,

pull, pound.
Stretch, fitful fusion, incubus-knock.

Dawn agony teething.

Days later when I first stood up,
I was a palsied crab, dazed.
Skittering, scraping.

Hot flurry of spindles
seeking ground. Ratchet, legs of

milk teeth, what moves
us on, gravity and shallow

grave. In the mirror I saw
my navel was nearly stretched down
to where my brown coat began.

Skin the color of dry pomegranate
pulsed at the suture.

I told my new body,
"You must die."

10   I began emitting more heat than ever.
Sporadically I shook.

8.

Once, only once,
I let him ride me
bareback. It was near sunset,

late, late November.
He had completed his day's work.
We were in the kitchen,

and he brushed away
a housefly from the veins
along my numb legs.

I kneeled a bit.
He relaxed into my back.
He held onto my neck,

his calves against my flanks,
and I started for the field,
what felt like an ocean.

There's a trust
that won't throw us.
He understood:

no bridle, no reins.

11

II.

Low Tide on the Windward Shore

Orange starfish and wood pilings brought me here,

where nets have mangled eels
and my heel is tarred and aching.

Where the imagined god's voice consoles me,
a vision of turtle eggs torn open,

sewn up imperfectly—
I break shells with my feet.

May I swim past the reefline to freedom.

15

Promiscuity

A starling skims
the chlorinated pool and touches
the water once.
I swat a housefly
that bit me like a horsefly.
I think of wholeness,
the summer sky that stays white
because of field fires and a hot,
weak southern wind;
parrotfish, which never close
their eyes; and the saint's eyes on the dish
that look deeply into my living carcass,
chapped and scoliosed,
that study the urethral flap,
its soiled membrane.
This morning there were dreams I misremembered
and wrote in a book.

And the hydrovac goes on cleaning the pool's bottom
while its dead float
in plain view,
mostly hornets in fetal positions
and nondescript flies.
It's unable to complete
its task and rest,
like my love for that desolate
beach or this figurine
that I hold in the sun.
Must I look at him again—
tied to the same chipped
column and orange-red
from the lashing?
How many times did I reach into those waves
for a broken cowrie to scrape
the tar off my feet?

I must stop thinking
about my heart.
I'll make a thread of myself.
Shed bones. And fat and lust.
Taper into floss, fiber optics,
a pure line of dreaming
and attention.
Then spider morning-mesh.

One of the Magi

Buggy baby, the Thou
in the deep feedbox

that rams snort around,
I'm shaking a vial

of my fragrant
blood. Other resin's

in my tatty pockets.
O Mumsy and "Dad"

and you donkeys braying
toward Aries and Vero Beach,

you hogs inhaling
half-thawed Swanson slops—

clear the barn, he's
mine. I see his unhealed

wound, a fresh
umbilical stump

that purses and dilates
so urgently.

Do I unstopper,
pour, and smear?

Gift him everything
human, myrrhed virus?

18

Renunciation

When I stopped at some birches
along the path,

shivers came and went.

Images of him passed like a flat river barge:
reaching under my shirt

as we crouched in the necropolis,
carving open a watermelon
in our primitive kitchen.

There was ice on some junipers;
it was too warm for ice.

I felt thwarted.

I was gathering speed.

Brother on Brother

1.

A jay landing in wire grass,
the tiki hut's floor of wet tar—

prickly pears strung
on a line, blurred and gummy—

then cast on my wall,
the silhouette of a branch

drifting, after-air
of the opening door.

My skin, inescapable.
Outstretched on my belly,

I held onto the raised
stitching of the bedspread.

Waking from a dream,
I knew those were your

hands stealing away
and the laughing.

2.

Red lights, smeared,
wobbling in a circle:

they hung over me, materializing
from a cloud or thicket:

flesh, long-enfolded,
was unflapped:

the sour smell of
moist grooves exposed.

What leapt inside me
when the bell's mallet struck wetly

against my palette?
Who could stop the ringing?

Afterwards I made a plan
to escape the bitter drops:

I'd sleep with my face
in a pillow and try

to eat the fibers.
I'd be immovable.

3.

You watched over me;
sandpaper, gorge—

fold fallow plow.
Whispered, "I could kill you."

Reuben on Joseph

I should have snuffed him out
in his crib. Instead, through the bars,
I often pinched him.
He was my baby,
no one else's,
and he couldn't pinch back.

In the backyard, underneath the birdbath,
there's a pit that's my cistern.
Don't ask me how.
I want a deeper one, hidden
by the camellias, not for rain
but for housing him.
They'll think he's dead and mourn.

Late afternoons, pretending I'm fetching
water for my tub, I'll go feed him.
Brush his hair, stick his chained paw
with a scissor, I'll have used it already for
voicebox surgery—
he won't be able to cry out. And I'll read
him erotic stories, Bobbsey Twins,
Hardy Boys. I'll trace my
cursive Q's, uppercase,
on his flat stomach to impress him,
keeping him awake
so he can't play possum.

I'll show him what I learned
in the Okefenokee—I went there with a boy
collecting plants that catch flies
in their sticky little mouths.
When we were slogging alone, the kid breathed
warmly into the crotch of my pants.
I stopped beside a cypress. Then

bit back. Later, on my stomach,
the stirring, it felt familiar.

Before the first lesson, if he resists,
I'll dig my nails into his throat
but not deeply:
the tissue will be tender
from the stitches. I'll put spit
on my ears and his
to cool them, we'll be angry and hot.
(I've found it stops the ticks from
burrowing there and talking
in feminine voices, calling me gay—
I hear things.)
Then we'll be ready. I wonder
what I'll think about, my mouth
on his nape.

      I'm not ashamed
I hate him. I have every right.
Once he followed me down the driveway
to the leaf-choked gutter.
Water was rushing up the curb
of the cul-de-sac, spilling onto the sidewalk.
At the edge of the flood,
he took my left hand into his, kissed it,
as if I were a princess about to board a swanboat.
We kicked the wet debris
and laughed until our sitter called us inside.
He hasn't kissed me since.
He'll never stand above me at night
to stare at my sleeping body
and record what I say in my sleep.

Pontiff

He lowers his blessing
mushroom-capped   glistening
and traces the trinity

      Axilla   (overturned skullcap)

        Areola   (fisherman's ring, still warm)

          Perineum   (the grating whispered through)

Even this   his infallible arc
drawn in clear finish   can't enter
the scuffed depths of heaven

Self-Portrait as Robert Mapplethorpe

Those shit-dribbles?
They're Scratch's fault,
my sick pet monkey.

When you're gone, I'll lysol
my apartment's altars,
wipe them with Veronica's rag.

For now you're the latest offering—
for the cloven-footed one,
I just cleaved you farther

at your opening, the spidery,
pink star gone nova, I
wanted you to feel

what I felt at sixteen, the tearing
and glow in my stomach
when I breathed across

a magazine in cellophane
and watched it cloud up.
Another hazy Adonis

who couldn't be mine.
Later, yes, many others—in a patrolled
park, on the pier.

This is liberation?
You and I are closer now,
bound together without rope,

with pain, pure trust.
Sex, the only thing
worth living for;

for a minute, reaching into you,
I forgot I was human,
that I was at all—

am, am, am!
My orchids over there
talk about Warhol's hair.

Their neon yellow lips,
where pollinators
ought to land, wag on

and on about my swollen
glands, my torso-rash—
it is the prophet's new

26

mantle, my names
escape from speckled
pistils, throats, I'm told

what to do, I don't do it, and then?

Manger

I'm away in a manger, Sir—
swaddled in velveteen, gassy.

Father, father, please bother.
Burp me hard and again.

I'm a moist larva struggling
in the haylessness,

squirming against the trough's grain,
right into new splinters.

You're so post-pupa—
winged, sparkly,

breaded. It's quake and
take, I help:

you hold my hand, use
my mouth of little O's.

You're a post-partum
wrangler, I'm the long-awaited

calf still soggy—
pluck and drive me.

Mako Man, thrash me,
your fat, unhappy seal pup

in the cove. I'm
mildness, lurch—you're starting it

once more, that wrist-
action—yet, about,

for. Bring the binky closer,
sing of joy, leather.

Make me. I'm freckles,
yogurt, resounding.

Circumcision

1. Numbed

Such rawness and nada.
Am below him.

Surges of feeling.
Unscrews the jar

of cream. Twirl and flick
of his. Greasy end

tipped toward me.
Better. Am ready.

Stop the racing.
Shear off the seething

suckers. Am antsy starfish.
On a mirror above a mirror.

2. Cutting Away

in one life   was a narwhal   fed a starving Inuit village
in another   a tapeworm   peeking out   was tugged out diced

in a temple with breathing tubes   blooming 8th day—
taste it   my heart having made it good   for my father/Father

3. Afterworld

My clipped cuticles, my foreskin: they did not follow me into the grave. Or fly
back to me when I woke in it and walked up the staircase, which had unhinged
itself and sprung up farther than I could see. Ascending without appetite, I heard
my scars muttering, describing his look of suppressed desire upon me as a child,
and wondered if when I arrived, winded, He would finally touch me where he
had wanted to.

III.

Virus

1.

It slept for seven years
underneath my father's sheets.

It slept for seven
years, wakes to far-off thunder,
a kettle's faint cry.

Its mouth is parched, ringed
with teeth like a lamprey.

It was afloat with reverie,
now it's pacing the hard floor.

In these rooms at the end
of a cul-de-sac,
why did it choose him and not me?

2.

Lovely he appeared
      to me, with a gash under
his nipple. Suddenly the slit
      I had desired to thrust into.

Only he saw me entering him,
      eagerly, with my finger.
—How could I stop myself? Ecstasy,
      how I've made a faith of you.

3.

The staph infection on the inside

of his thigh persisted, a field of red poppies
unable to wither.

No, lighter—the rose
meat of a starfish, its nubs

but tinier. Fire polyps that gave
to the touch.

4.

I sat in the chair,
half-listening to him,

staring at the pockmarked door,
its watery peephole.

"You're going to get it."

The motel curtain
was a bride's veil;

light slowed
into sheer waves.

"You're going to."

I counted new
splotches on his forehead.
Islands cooling

into an archipelago?
"You're going to get it too," my father told me.

"There's no way you won't—"

Pale bags under
his eyes
bunched slightly.

On both sides of the bed
his boxes were stacked.

5.

Daddybody, why do I want to inhabit you?
Shoreline cliffs still call out
for the continent that broke away.

From here, my gums can't taste your skin.
Why deny me scabs and leather?
The ears of my bunny hat droop.
Lie down on the grass you've mown.

Hold me there so I ride your breathing.
Warp me with your heat, nip me
with your barbed, crinkle-cut
hairs. I promise not to ball up like a pillbug.

No, you be still. Let me unbuckle you,

find your tight portal,
and discover what you ate.

37

6.

Facing the idle power plant,
we fished the lagoon
from a concrete wall.

Before we cast, you taught me
where to hook a shrimp
so it wouldn't tear free:

under the horn on the top
of its head, between the two brains,
away from the fluttering gills . . .

Coastal pines blew,
the red bobber dove.
I struggled to reel in the line,

my small arms shaking.
A stingray bolted up,
flapping its wings in the air

as I lowered the pole to the ground.
Sandaled foot on barbed tail,
you took my hand.

You ran it along the drab back—

7.

To lose my father
I walked the road.

After a hot night of no wind.
One planet fading.

Withered orchard,
cloudy light.
A sprinkler, chugging
and returning.
Up to the right,
on a monastery wall, the face
of a frescoed saint,
all but a jawline
chipped away.
Initials scratched into
his faint bloodied gown. A fissure
across his book.

8.

at Keats' grave

Staring at the stone
can't bore a wormhole to you.
My right heel burns,
the other calf asleep,
from crossing my legs;
I try to shake off flies
and the sadness
knotted in my shoulders:
my father would clear his throat three times
before speaking to us at dinner,
like the last several spasms of a ladyfish.
O to enter his mouth
and not stop there,
to stake out the great stopping lung.

9.

Sitting in brown grass,
I touch the drop

about to fall from the berry.
The grit in my nail remains.

What flow,
what know,

are shivers across the dry,
cut lip of morning,

the river that curves
with the field.

Ice is
hardly ice.

The world's a blinding basin,
wakefulness

in a fever dream—he said
he touched her because

it felt good.
I hold the low holly branch,

shake it of melted snow
against the hide

of an imagined fawn.
The child milked him dry

as his knees rocked
her bedframe. The groan

and the rocking.
Because it felt good.

10.

Scattering the relics
from my satchel,

I wandered scrubby hills.

A jay's song echoed
through boulders.

I placed his tongue,

white like wedding cake,
on a dry turkey-oak leaf.

To touch and be touched,

we've both entered rooms.
As his balls slapped

against someone, he prayed.

Just outside a tortoise burrow—
that's where I left his dick.

Wrinkled clown.

Rolled opiate.
Fallen toy pillar blazing

in the night at the end

of the century. At the edge
of those palmettos,

where I held a shovel.

11.

On a pitch-pine night,
in a marsh emptied of water,
I too met beauty:

entering a man
without latex—tighter, cloudier
than the clear mantle

of the holy child
who stares from a parapet.
I felt no pain, no guilt,

his legs held up the firmament,
which the airport's beacon
lit across like

heat lightning,
his eyes flashing
with that rhythm

and mine.
All that remained for me
to break through

was the skin around his heart.

12.

Startled by the pealing beep
of his text, leaving my rolling chair
for his waterbed, I'm his newest
Internet bride. My belly's
down, my back's waxed. My lean,
starved womb's
a slight rectal bloom. My rinsed-out
entrails are surely rife with
micro-cuts. So easily he works
into me like a duck driving its bill
through retention-pond mire.
He finishes and I'm warm.
Am I carrying his self-replicating child?

13.

In the center of my father's still-life,
the gutted ray hung on a hook.
The underside was a bloodstained

door, the mouth almost
pleased. He wanted to forget
everything he had seen. All we had done.

14.

maid of Odysseus and Penelope

Even before seeing the scar on his thigh,
I knew he was my master, disguised—
never forget the scent of a boy you've nursed.

He looked at me like a weary otter.
Lowering his heel into the basin,
he threatened to choke me if I told them

he was home. So I thumbed a knot
in his arch, hummed, kept washing—
he confided he'd nearly died twice,

neuropathy was spreading in his feet;
he didn't want a wife any more. I felt pity,
not compassion, for the family.

Downstairs a saucer shattered
on the kitchen floor. Suitors ate his food.

IV.

Do you suppose yourself advancing on real ground toward a real heroic man?
Have you no thought O dreamer that it may be all maya, illusion?
—Walt Whitman, "Are You the New Person Drawn Toward Me?"

Thirteen Labors

1. Retrospection in Hannibal, Missouri
[FIRST LABOR]

Here at the foot of Cardiff Hill
where Tom and Huck played, in the shadow
of their bronze

statues, gulls shrieking
from the closing dealership to the river's
island—here we can't search for

that jpeg of your left hand
on my throat, the other pinching
my jugular and twisting.

Which one of us, in that shot
with now-eroded Atlantic dunes
backed by scrub, was the fissure,

49

healed then reopened
unintentionally? We were
diapered in extrasolar light,

your feet held up
our sky. Or your lionback
shucked it of stars? Here we retell

our grim, uninteresting
legends. Here a steamboat docks for winter.
Here thanks for sinew,

winter, here firedint—through cloud.

2. Interactivity

[SECOND LABOR]

You and I press our naked bodies against the vast
touchscreen's glass—there's squeaking,
laughing—to make out
with our reflections, but the display

switches on, ending
our mirror. Now we're kissing the myth's playback,
another boy, low-resolution, who's
about to cauterize a hydra's decapitation wound
with a firebrand that our thrusts

and smooches—scattering the cursor—
drag into the swamp. Deadly gall
leaking. Self-regenerating heads. We make
the land crab pinch off the hero's leg
at the knee. Suspended above it all,

we're kicking. Pressed so close
that heroism and loss are
abstracted, alterable, we'll enter, almost, what's
roiling beneath us, blurred.

3. Detainment

In the undisclosed desert facility, they strapped me to a steel table and told me to recite the poem that would save the world.

(I arrived there in a windowless, automated van driven inside the hollow mountain.

Through the forest they chased me to exhaustion.)

They polished metal tools I'd never seen before.

To break me down, at first one of them kept tapping on my nose and whispering lyrics, access codes, rapid sequences of Greek letters and English surnames.

One tried to interface with my brain, injecting a sort of horned electrode into Wernicke's, then Broca's. My larynx in spasm. My hands were hooves, nightingale beaks, the fluorescent tubes above me were my white bones.

I chanted baby names during sensations of drowning, overwhelming nausea. Back and forth from ice-cold water, mock burials. They crowned me with electrified laurels.

51

They touched me, laughing.

They touched me and I sang and for what?

52

4. Mindfulness

[FOURTH LABOR]

There's no grave enclosed with a silver fence
because I've never had a body,
never been illustrated in an acid-free

book of books. I pass through
folded laundry, every hesitant keystroke—
the entire experiment, humanity,

for now continuing—and look
and look at you, through you, feeling nothing,
all the deck hands scrambling to restore

steering to the rudderless vessel
glued inside the sideways bottle.
Your shallow breathing's neither bad nor good.

Join me here, in the untherapeutic
everywhere, and see the futility
of revision, self-promotion.

Of going on about freedom,
the holographic boar you try to net
and subdue in the snow.

5. Self-Portrait As Cindy Sherman

[FIFTH LABOR]

I don't recognize myself in this C-print from 1990
      that I've scanned and photoshopped,
the contrast adjusted
      so that blood stains
in the lionskin—all I was wearing, a costume
      bought at a Roman flea market—

have faded. Sepia's control
      slider manipulated only a little,
the image now
      more like an Old Master's
in oils. I added
      a Tigris goose feather

behind my left ear, old prayer
      rugs copied, pasted
as the draping background. No lit candle,
      no dish of dried figs.
I pose like the 9/11 pundit
      photographed last week in Battery Park

for his book jacket, not a hero
      contemplating how to clear dung
from a king's stable. I grip
      a bowling pin spray-painted
umber, it's my club—here
      on the monitor, see

my prosthetic triceps
      bulging, my rubber torso rippling
in the window light?
      I cropped the window.
See the furrows etched into
      my putty-brow? I pretend focus,

pain. I have disappeared
        into this crusade—I'm Hercules,
he's Hercules, with my

        greenish eyes. Is this shot
worth saving?

6. Simulation

[SIXTH LABOR]

Moonlight fizzy
across the reedy lake, halogen
lamplight reflecting off
the monitor, my 3D avatar yawns
on his tiny beach.
Pops his stiff neck
and spine. A two-second lag
and I imitate him in my desk chair.
Soon he'll be asleep.
Clacking castanets,
he scared thousands of swimming geese
into flight, shooting them
out of the sky, each carcass
deleted as it fell.

Months ago, one foggy solstice,
I programmed him
to have my brown hair
but long curls,
my cough but perfect teeth,
nipples always hard.
Broad, even shoulders.
He's shorter, brawnier,
saved to a drive. He walks
without blinking, with
blazing purpose—
and I'm distracted, hungry,
aching all over.
I wear more than just a lionskin.

7. First Contact

You loom over me, you burn
above, a cigar-shaped mothership scorching my tuft.
I'm the Show-Me-State farmer immobilized by you.
When you're done with me, there's missing time,
a deep scoop-mark or three on my thigh.
A tracking device throbs below my hairline.

Our double-sided toys return to their drawer.
You and I febreze your pillowtop,
tawny as raw cane sugar, and the box
springs, the ottoman where we began.
The smell of pug-waste lingers.
We make the bed, I see your happy trail's

braided like Saturn's F-ring, and your beard-body,
at the sternum, has a hairless
dish where you receive millions
of frequencies from the Milky Way—I sort
through them, wirelessly,
for the breakthrough signal. Just one chord
of ancient song. I also listen for signs of death.

57

8. 134,700+ Views

Replay the clip of two horses, Petty
and Portia, eating their master.
(Wipe the LCD with your sleeve.
You and I compromised on the angle of the screen.)
Unmute their long, wet inhales.
Their smacking, their audible relief, an iguana in the rafters.
The master's useless apologies, stammered.
For keeping them stabled in filth.
Chained to bronze feeding-troughs.
Slow or pause at his final gesture.
An arm-stump swung
toward the crab set in the sky.

9. Lucid Spooning

[FLOATING LABOR]

1. Emanation

      bodiless at last,
I hold, flow,
      hear myself conspiring

to be several things:
      1) a sheepdog—stroke
her face, lower yourself

      to kiss her, she barks
lame thunder, headbutts you,
      bruising your nose's

misshapen bridge   2) ruddy eagle scouts
      hesitating to spoon
in your torn pup tent, hoping

      their rations last
till the search party arrives
      3) the dried bodies

of desert insects crushed
      for your cake frosting's
patriotic red dye   I ask myself

      why I'm so divided,

2. Awakening

      why I push against
what I don't know
      I'm bare and responsive, nothing's

choreographed and it's all
        unstoppable   I pulse
where I pulse, call it goodness

        or I'm still armored:
there's security to consider,
        efficiency, withstanding

rejection   your gray eyes

60

10. Monogamy

[NINTH LABOR]

Big bluestem and slough grass brushing against his sunburned neck and unusually long arm hair, he walks the mowed path through the center, toward the fresh firebreaks, and imagines white smoke, the slow crawl of an ignited line across the scrub. Tomorrow, if the high pressure system stays put and the wind is flat, park officials will set fire to the seventy-four acres along the gravel road, a controlled burn of the last remaining prairie in the county. Last night, typing into the blue-framed chat window for hours, he and a stranger wrote—back and forth, all in lowercase—an elaborate story involving belts and their bodies.

11. Detainment

[TENTH LABOR]

Tear down this firewall. Open
attachments: a friend's poem, full of birds
and trees, afraid of wordiness
then astringency; an illegally distributed song;
spreadsheets of debts, your recurring
payments. Save, save the video of his hanging.
Of their 7/7/07 beachside wedding.

Turn off the machines. Gather,
scatter your belongings—you're escorted
from the National Museum
to a cramped, swiffered cell. Your sketch,
from memory, of an amphora's painted
cattle, those cows outside
in the courtyard, this piped-in voice, it's all 0s and 1s.

12. Marriage

[ELEVENTH LABOR]

opened book set
on glass: versos (you)

rectos (me) spit out
warm at 600 x 600 dpi—

btw it's false & crazymaking
choosing between virtue

& pleasure: let's dissect
our pitcher plant's

pouch before Dec.
dormancy & sort carcasses:

paper wasp silken tofu
autumn's gnat—

collated automatically
stapled we have "eternity":

Hesperian tree pulp
plus butterwort lube for

guardian serpent: we're
climbed left to right

63

13. Portrait of My Greyhound
As Cerberus

[TWELFTH LABOR]

We're about to leave.
Up through cold grotto
to floodlit earth. He emits sounds,

neither growls nor whimpers.
I frontline
his spine, peter pan his tongues.

His three needlenoses,
working the air that rushes
from the gate, drip

with clear snot, each nostril
a tiny mouth murmuring a list of ways
to violate a man.

What is a soul?

Before fitting him with a tight collar,
after striking him
into near-stillness, I stroke

one pair of his ears.

V.

Ascent

I surrendered my butane lighter to you at the gate—
but not my pigeon, not my raisinet heart in four pieces.

Explosives lined my lung, you
defused them. You tore my ticket.

Now you're miming how to fasten
a seat belt, but I—giraffe-scruffy, dehydrated,

love-starved—am already strapped in,
tray table up. Sputter,

growl, groan and fire, fire, we're flying on a globe
of cloud above the dying, lit-up

city, into wind shear, geese, BB-sized hail—
my briefing card says our exits

have inflatable slides, the cushions
float. You and I fly and rattle.

Camphor

Being is enough,
it's so bright

and at the verge—of
creation, of mixing

cardinal red
and baby's breath

to regain the smell of her camphor,
the feel of silver

wrapped in black felt.
Here much is glinting and sharp;

there are recoveries,
disappearances.

Here I speak to my longing for live oaks,
not bodies.

Prayer at Ojai

I asked the deliverer of mountains,
the leaper of straits,

to bring you to the citrus groves
where I sleep and sing in the heat;

or to the river that I walk along,
now just algae and smooth stones,

an abandoned bicycle on the banks.

When you never came,
I asked him to give me a sick gelding to ride

from one ocean to the other,
to your books and sandals.

—There it is again,
the brawling above my stomach.

My throat closing.

Mother of Light

Wading into the water
with a dip net,

she wanted to show me the brown,
flitting larvae

of dragonflies.
Like a river's chop half-deflected

by a piling, memories
returned as she kneeled:

orange starfish in turtle grass;
the jewel wrapped in cloth,

hidden across the chaotic town
for me to retrieve;

the lanterns of
the night-fishers, offshore—

Revision

One day he'll reach for our shelved book,
silver worn off spine. So he can read

himself at arm's length,

I've switched every pronoun.
Let marsh smoke gathering before dawn

wake him
under that old cypress in my dream:

"Your words didn't change me,"
he says at my nape,

occipital to coccyx,
a starry, murky stream;

on the muddy bank
we're naked

and stare past one another—
let there be no silences.
We swim to where the water

slows, trembles,

the moment blown into glass,
held and broken.

South of Jacksonville

Four shrimp boats on the horizon. Receding squall,
clear winter sea.
Walking the tide line,

I hear his voice again,

pained,
full of resolve.

The lagoon where
blue starfish flicker,

curl—I'll follow him there.

Three Attempts at Understanding

1.

A birdcall and a breath in the roofless chapel:
that pleasure was brief.

Unlike one full rotation of this galaxy.
Or sycamores peeling along the river,

guilt fanning out through my
body, is enlightenment accidental?

Like red pear slice, dry mouth.

2.

This life—this one—
is a fleck of yolk
on a cooling skillet.

After so much,
I can rest?

3.

The ground under me damp
with early snowmelt, my
craving diminishes,

diminishes,
grows—die back,
return, die back,

die back—it surges
in my mind

toward a body other than his:
robins feeding; orange

breeds orange against
brown world. Snow only
at the north foot of

each tree. I'm dappled inside
with sunlight.

And then I'm not.

Onto

A dead man
tethered to a dead horse

steps onto the island,
having waded across the shallow channel

luminous with rushing coins.

They enter the abandoned armory,
its main room.
Lining the sills are cuttlebones.

And pelican bones?
His eyes shut,

the horse's open,
sunlight blazing across the ruined floor—
doorframe, no,

windowframe, water.

Notes

"Centaur": The terms "ilia," "ischia," and "pubis" are
the three main bones of the pelvis. "Utthita Trikonasana"
is the Sanskrit word for the triangle pose in yoga.

"Brother on Brother": The italicized words are taken
from Gerard Manley Hopkins's "Pied Beauty."

"Self-Portrait as Robert Mapplethorpe": I am indebted to Patricia Morrison's
Mapplethorpe: A Biography (Random House, 1995) and Richard Howard and
Ingrid Sischy's essays in *Robert Mapplethorpe* (Whitney Museum, 1988).

In the fourth section, I follow the order of Herakles' labors in Apollodoros'
Library of Mythology: (1) retrieve the hide of the Nemean lion; (2) kill the Lernaian
hydra; (3) capture the Keryneian hind; (4) capture the Erymanthian boar; (5) clean
the dung from the Augeian stables; (6) remove the Stymphalian water birds;
(7) capture the Cretan bull; (8) capture the horses of Diomedes; (9) retrieve the
belt of the Amazon Hippolyte; (10) steal Geryon's cattle; (11) retrieve
some of the Hesperides' apples; and (12) capture Cerberus.

"Mindfulness": The first line paraphrases Marianne Moore's
note to her poem "When I Buy Pictures."

"Marriage": The abbreviation "dpi" refers to dots per inch,
a measure of printer resolution.

"Portrait of My Greyhound as Cerberus": The word "frontline" refers to the brand of
canine flea-control medication; "peter pan" refers to the brand of peanut butter.

"Ascent" is for Andy Wiese.

"Mother of Light" is dedicated in memory of Dipa Ma (1911–1989).

The Brittingham Prize in Poetry

Ronald Wallace, *General Editor*

A Field Guide to the Heavens • Frank X. Gaspar
Robert Bly, Judge, 1999

A Path between Houses • Greg Rappleye
Alicia Ostriker, Judge, 2000

Horizon Note • Robin Behn
Mark Doty, Judge, 2001

Acts of Contortion • Anna George Meek
Edward Hirsch, Judge, 2002

The Room Where I Was Born • Brian Teare
Kelly Cherry, Judge, 2003

Sea of Faith • John Brehm
Carl Dennis, Judge, 2004

Jagged with Love • Susanna Childress
Billy Collins, Judge, 2005

New Jersey • Betsy Andrews
Linda Gregerson, Judge, 2007

Meditations on Rising and Falling • Philip Pardi
David St. John, Judge, 2008

Bird Skin Coat • Angela Sorby
Marilyn Nelson, Judge, 2009

The Mouths of Grazing Things • Jennifer Boyden
Robert Pinsky, Judge, 2010

Wait • Alison Stine
Cornelius Eady, Judge, 2011

Darkroom • Jazzy Danziger
Jean Valentine, Judge, 2012

Centaur • Greg Wrenn
Terrance Hayes, Judge, 2013